D0186018

Exploring CANALS

Daniel Nunn

raintree
a Capstone company — publishers for children

Raintree is an imprint of Capstone Global Library Limited, a company incorporated in England and Wales having its registered office at 264 Banbury Road, Oxford, OX2 7DY – Registered company number: 6695582

www.raintree.co.uk
myorders@raintree.co.uk

Edited by Helen Cox Cannons
Designed by Dynamo Limited
Original illustrations © Capstone Global Library Limited 2019
Picture research by Dynamo Limited
Production by Laura Manthe
Originated by Capstone Global Library Limited
Printed and bound in India

ISBN 978 1 4747 7449 9
22 21 20 19 18
10 9 8 7 6 5 4 3 2 1

British Library Cataloguing in Publication Data
A full catalogue record for this book is available from the British Library.

Acknowledgements
We would like to thank the following for permission to reproduce photographs: Alamy: Canals and boating UK, 18, 19, DT Images, 28 Top Right, Dunroamin Photography, 6, ImagesEurope, 20, Jeff Gilbert, 28 Bottom Left, Martin Fowler, 21, Peter Titmuss, 10 Bottom Left, 10 Bottom Right, Stephen Sykes, 15, Steve Bentley, 23; Getty Images: DigitalVision Vectors/filo, Design Element, E+/ChuckSchugPhotography, 26 (hard rushes), iStock Editorial/AlecOwenEvans, 26 (cormorant), iStock Editorial/Andyworks, 27 (dragonfly), iStock Editorial/asmithers, 26 (heron), iStock Editorial/Bebedi, 26 (coot), iStock Editorial/CaronB, 27 (trout), iStock Editorial/Choker, 27 (carp), iStock Editorial/cwk15, 27 (grass snake), iStock Editorial/DamianKuzdak, 26 (moorhen), iStock Editorial/David Muscroft, 26 (swan), iStock Editorial/Dgwildlife, 26 (kingfisher), iStock Editorial/HelenWalkerz65, 26 (duck), 27 (water vole), iStock Editorial/Ian_Redding, 27 (newt), iStock Editorial/Ieuan, 9, iStock Editorial/JanMiko, 27 (pond skater), iStock Editorial/jpa1999, 27 (perch), iStock Editorial/ jremes84, 26 (goose), iStock Editorial/MarkGillow, 27 (otter), iStock Editorial/MikeLane45, 27 (shrew), iStock Editorial/Nicola Warburton, 27 (butterfly), iStock Editorial/Paolo Paradiso, 24, iStock Editorial/RichardHayman13, 14, iStock Editorial/Rixipix, 27 (damselfly), iStock Editorial/SteveAllenPhoto, 7, iStock Editorial/toddtaulman, 26 (water-lily), iStock Editorial/Viesinsh, 27 (toad), iStock/BerndBrueggemann, 22, iStock/ELIKA, 29, iStock/Jrleyland, Cover Bottom Right, iStock/KHellon, 13, Keystone, 12, Paul Quayle, 16, Photononstop/Eurasia Press, 1, 25, SSPL/Past Pix, 8, UIG/Education Images, 11, 17; Shutterstock: D. Pimborough, Cover Middle, S-F, 4, Thomas Marchhart , Cover Bottom Left, Yorkman, 5.

Contents

Some words are shown in bold, **like this**. You can find out what they mean by looking in the glossary.

What are canals?

People have travelled and transported things along rivers for thousands of years. Centuries ago, people were able to travel faster by boat than on roads. This was because the roads were terrible and everything had to be pulled by horse! It was much easier to carry large, heavy loads by boat than by horse and cart.

There have been boats on large rivers like the Thames in London since Roman times.

The Leeds and Liverpool Canal is an example of a man-made waterway. It took workers 46 years to build it.

The problem with rivers is that they don't always go where you need them to! To get round this, people came up with the idea of building canals. A canal is like a river but is man-made. The canal is dug out of the ground then filled with water so that boats can travel along it.

A new transport network

Horses walked along special paths that run alongside the canals. These are called towpaths.

Most canals in Britain were built in the 1700s and early 1800s. During this time, there were lots of improvements in **manufacturing** and **industry**. This period in history became known as the Industrial Revolution. Canal boats were used to carry **raw materials** to and from **factories**. Most boats were pulled by horses or donkeys.

The Bridgewater Canal

The Bridgewater Canal is often called England's first canal. Opened in 1761, it was named after its owner, the Duke of Bridgewater. The Duke built the canal to move coal from his **mines** at Worsley to factories and **mills** in Manchester. In 1776, the canal was **extended** to Runcorn, where it joined the River Mersey. This meant goods could be carried from Manchester to Liverpool. There they could be shipped across the world from Liverpool's famous **port**.

Ingenious engineering

Creating a canal was very hard work. Workers had to cut their way through the ground using picks, shovels and wheelbarrows. Once they had dug out the canal channel, it was lined with clay to stop the water from leaking out. Then sheep and cows were marched along the bottom of the canal to press the clay down!

Canal workers were known as "navvies" (short for "navigators"). These navvies are building the Manchester Ship Canal in 1890.

This is a lock on the Kennet and Avon Canal. The lock separates two different stretches of water.

One big problem for canal builders was how to get boats up and down hills. The answer was to create **locks**. A lock is a small **chamber** with gates at each end. It is like a water lift for boats! A lock joins two stretches of water that are at different heights.

Moving through locks

To make a boat go up from one level of the canal to a higher level, the lock is filled with water. To make a boat go down, the lock is emptied. Boaters wind up **paddles** at either end of the lock to let the water in or out. Then they push the lock gates open and the boat can move forward.

In the left-hand picture, a narrowboat is at the bottom of a lock waiting to go up. In the right-hand picture, the paddles have been opened and the lock has filled with water.

Caen Hill locks

Caen Hill locks on the Kennet and Avon Canal in Wiltshire is one of the longest **flight** of locks in the country. There are 29 locks in total over a distance of 3.2 kilometres (2 miles). Together, the locks raise the canal by more than 72 metres (237 feet) in height. At its steepest point, there are 16 locks all in a row, one straight after the other. It usually takes a boat between 5 and 6 hours to travel through all 29 locks.

Tunnelling through

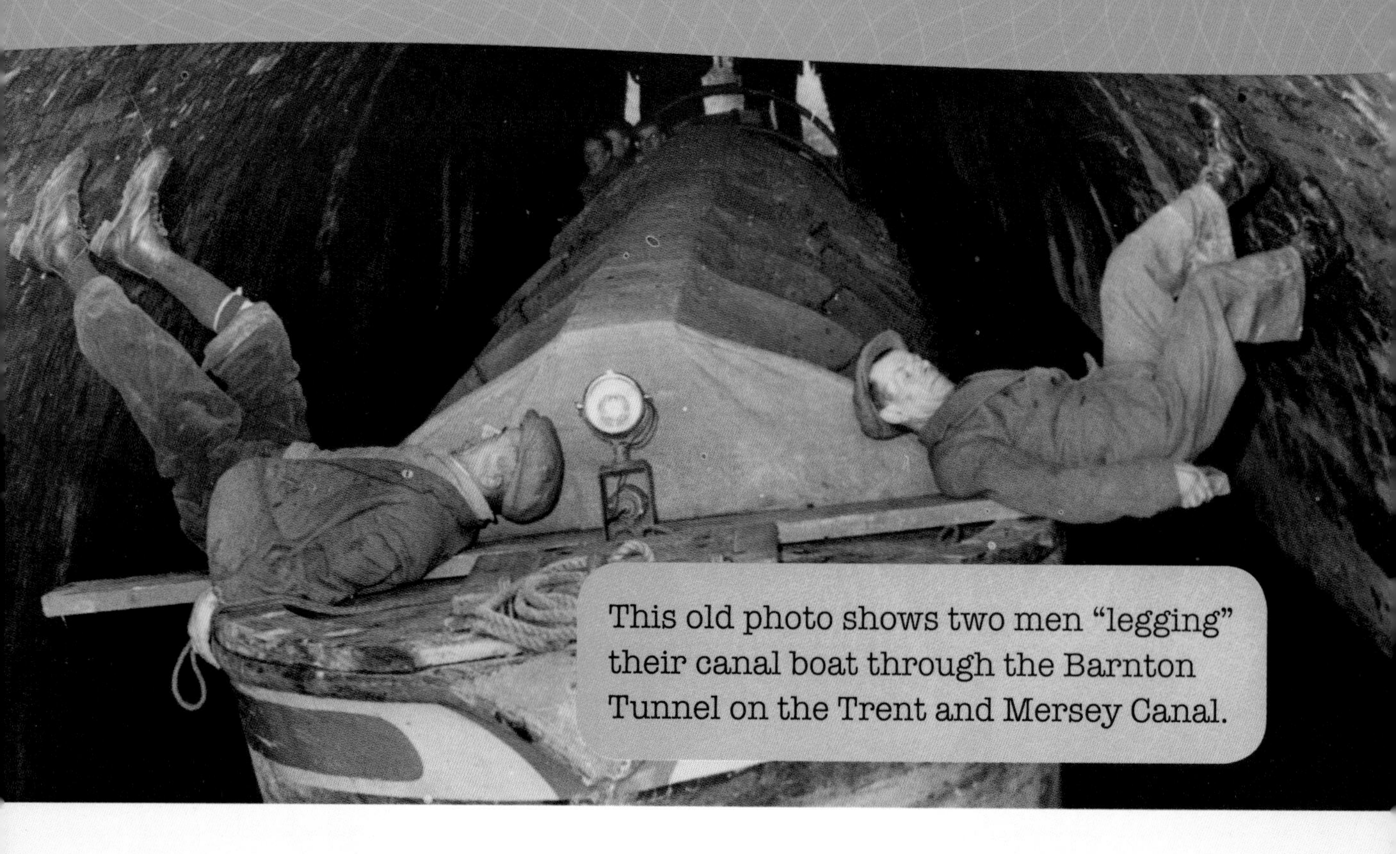

This old photo shows two men "legging" their canal boat through the Barnton Tunnel on the Trent and Mersey Canal.

Sometimes canal builders had to dig tunnels straight through hills because they could not build up or around them. Travelling through a narrow tunnel by boat was not easy. The only way of moving the boat through was if two people lay across the front of the boat and "walked" along the sides of the tunnel. This was called "legging".

Standedge Tunnel

Standedge Tunnel on the Huddersfield Narrow Canal in Yorkshire is Britain's longest and highest tunnel. It is also the deepest underground. The tunnel was first opened in 1811 and is 5.6 kilometres (3.5 miles) long. There is no towpath – boaters had to walk their horses over the top of the hill. They would meet up with their boats at the other end.

Amazing aqueducts and brilliant boatlifts

As well as tunnels, canal **engineers** built aqueducts to help canals and boats get through the countryside. Aqueducts are bridges that carry water across valleys, roads and rivers. The most famous canal aqueduct is the Pontcysyllte Aqueduct on the Llangollen Canal in Wales. It was opened in 1805. It carries boats over the River Dee along a thin **trough** of water.

This narrowboat is travelling along the Pontcysyllte Aqueduct. It is held up by 19 high arches.

The Falkirk Wheel lifts boats down from the Union Canal at the top, to the Forth and Clyde Canal at the bottom.

In other places, engineers built special "boatlifts". These were built to connect canals and rivers. The Anderton Boatlift was built in 1875. It links the Trent and Mersey Canal in Cheshire with the River Weaver. In Scotland, a brand new **rotating** boatlift was opened in 2002. It is called the Falkirk Wheel.

All about narrowboats

To be able to fit through locks on many canals, boats have to be no wider than 2.13 metres and no longer than 22 metres.

Many British canals are extremely narrow. They needed a special type of boat that was thin enough to fit through tunnels and **locks** – the narrowboat. Narrowboats carried all kinds of **cargo**, from coal and wood to chocolate. Famous chocolate makers Cadbury used narrowboats to carry cocoa and chocolate to and from their **factory** in Bourneville.

On working narrowboats, most of the space was needed for cargo. Living areas were small, often brightly painted cabins at one end of the boat. Very clever use was made of every inch of space. For example, doors folded down to become tables. Boats were **traditionally** decorated with roses and castles.

These are traditionally painted Buckby cans. They were used to store drinking water on top of the cabin.

Power and steering

In the late 1800s, companies started using steam engines in their narrowboats. This meant that boats could run day and night. However, the engine, boiler and coal needed to power them took up too much space. In the early 1900s, boats were built with gas engines. Then the switch to diesel engines was made. Today, nearly all narrowboats are powered by diesel engines.

This photo shows a diesel engine inside a narrowboat cabin.

On traditional narrowboats, the tiller is often painted in brightly-coloured stripes.

At the back of a narrowboat there is a small deck where the boat driver stands. The boat is steered using a long thin rod called a tiller. The tiller is connected to a **rudder** underneath the water. The rudder moves when the tiller is pushed or pulled in different directions.

Problems for the waterways

Unlike narrowboats, lorries can travel almost anywhere!

From the mid-1800s onwards, canals stopped being the favourite method of transport for goods. Railway tracks were built across Britain and trains began to take over. Trains were faster and cheaper to run than narrowboats and canals. Then, in the 1900s, roads were improved and cars and lorries were also used to carry goods.

Many people stopped using canals. Gradually, canals began to close and were even built over. In 1963, a particularly cold winter meant that all the remaining canals froze over. Narrowboats were unable to move along them. To keep their businesses going, many companies who still used canals were forced to switch to other methods of transport.

Long sections of the Thames and Severn Canal no longer contain any water.

Britain's canals today

Thankfully, this was not the end of the story for Britain's canals. During the late 20th century, many canals were **restored** by people who thought the canals were too special to be lost forever. Now, lots of people go on holiday on narrowboats and many canals have become **tourist** spots.

The Llangollen Canal in Wales is visited by many people because of the beautiful scenery there.

Huddersfield Narrow Canal

The Huddersfield Narrow Canal closed in 1944. It was **abandoned** for more than 50 years after this. Many people thought that it would be impossible to reopen – part of the canal had even been turned into a car park! After many years, the canal finally reopened in 2001. Now it is one of the most beautiful canals in the country, taking boaters across the Pennine Hills.

Canal holidays

There are lots of different ways to have fun at your local canal.

Many people go boating on canals because it is such a good way to relax. The speed limit is 4 miles per hour – you have no choice but to slow down! Canals make excellent holiday places for walkers and cyclists because of their long, flat towpaths. People also go canoeing and fishing on canals.

Some canals are at the heart of a local area. The city of Birmingham has more than 56 kilometres (35 miles) of canals running through it. That's more than the Italian city of Venice – and Venice is world-famous for canals! Shops, restaurants and museums line the waterside. Thousands of people visit every day.

Brindleyplace is a popular canal-side area of Birmingham. It is named after James Brindley (1716–1772), who was a famous canal engineer.

Waterways wildlife

Britain's canals are home to many different species of animals, birds, insects and plants. This includes more than 50 species of butterfly! How many of these plants and creatures can you spot on a visit to *your* local canal?

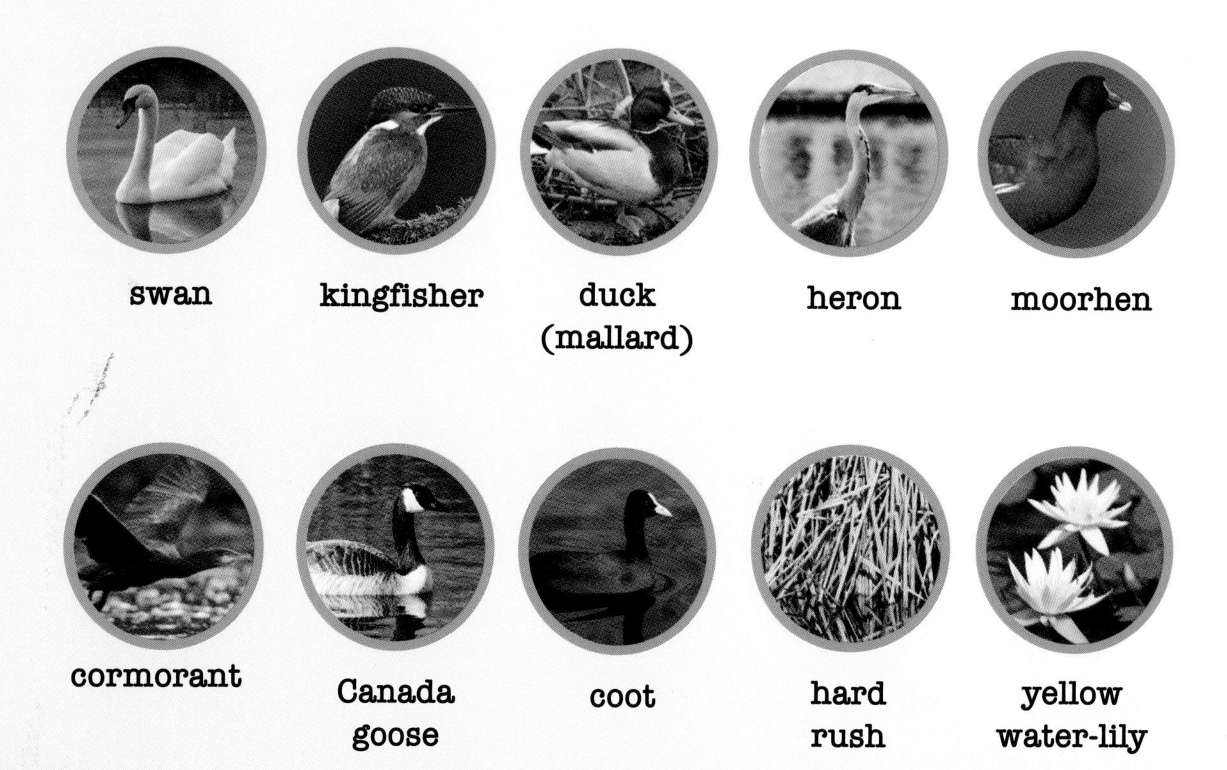

otter
shrew
water vole
grass snake
toad
newt
perch
carp
brown trout
butterfly
dragonfly
pond skater
damselfly

Boating top tips!

Thinking of going on a canal holiday? Here are a few top tips!

Feeding ducks is always fun but bread is not good for ducks. Instead, try feeding them corn, lettuce, peas, oats, bird seed or rice.

Every canal bridge has a number on it. You can use these to find out where you are on a canal map.

Stay safe near the water. Always wear a life jacket, especially if you are not a strong swimmer.

Stand well away from the edge of any **locks**. There can be very fast-flowing water and you could fall a long way down.

Know your narrowboat terms! The back of a boat is called the stern and the front is called the bow. The kitchen is called a galley and beds are called berths.

Map of Britain's canal network

This map shows the main canals and rivers that you can cruise by narrowboat in Great Britain.

Glossary

abandon give up completely
cargo goods carried on a boat
chamber compartment or small space
engineer person who uses science and maths to plan, design or build
extend make something longer
factory building where things are made
flight group word for more than one lock
industry business or trade
lock small section of water used to move boats up and down
manufacturing process of making something
mill building that has machines to grind grain into flour or meal
mine place underground where miners dig up minerals such as coal or gold
paddle block used to open and close a hole to let water into a lock
port town or city with a harbour where ships can load and unload cargo
raw materials natural things, such as wood or cotton, that are used to make something
restore repair or bring back something
rotate move round in a circle
rudder flat underwater object used to steer a boat
tourist someone who visits a place for fun
traditionally in a traditional way; in a way that people have done for many years
trough long, narrow channel of water

Find out more

Book

Canals and Dams! With 25 Science Projects for Kids (Explore Your World), Anita Yusada (Nomad Press, 2018)

Places to visit

London Canal Museum, London
www.canalmuseum.org.uk
At this museum you can find out more about the history of London's canals and boats. You can also learn about the people and horses that worked on them.

National Waterways Museum, Ellesmere Port
www.canalrivertrust.org.uk/places-to-visit/national-waterways-museum
This museum has a large collection of historic boats that you go on board to look at. You can also go on a boat trip.

National Waterways Museum, Gloucester
www.canalrivertrust.org.uk/places-to-visit/gloucester-docks
At this museum, find out all about Gloucester Docks and the Gloucester and Sharpness Canal.

The Canal Museum, Stoke Bruerne
www.canalrivertrust.org.uk/thecanalmuseum
Go on a journey through the stories and traditions of Britain's canals.

The Yorkshire Waterways Museum, Goole
www.waterwaysmuseum.org.uk/
Find out about the history and heritage of Yorkshire's waterways.

Index